PRINCEWILL LAGANG

Rebuilding Trust: Healing After Betrayal

First published by PRINCEWILL LAGANG 2023

Copyright © 2023 by Princewill Lagang

All rights reserved. No part of this publication may be reproduced, stored or transmitted in any form or by any means, electronic, mechanical, photocopying, recording, scanning, or otherwise without written permission from the publisher. It is illegal to copy this book, post it to a website, or distribute it by any other means without permission.

Princewill Lagang asserts the moral right to be identified as the author of this work.

First edition

This book was professionally typeset on Reedsy.
Find out more at reedsy.com

Contents

1	Introduction	1
2	Understanding Betrayal	3
3	The Importance of Trust	5
4	Taking Responsibility	8
5	Rebuilding Communication	10
6	Gaining Insight into Motivations	13
7	Setting Boundaries	16
8	Navigating Emotional Healing	19
9	Transparency and Honesty	22
10	Patience and Time	25
11	Chapter 11: Seeking Professional Help	27
12	The Journey of Renewed Trust	30

1

Introduction

Trust is a delicate thread that weaves the fabric of our relationships, forming the basis upon which we build connections, intimacy, and understanding with others. But what happens when that thread is torn, when trust is shattered by betrayal? This is the question at the heart of our journey in this book, as we explore the intricate process of rebuilding trust after it has been broken.

In the world of human relationships, betrayal can take on many forms – from the devastating breach of infidelity to the quieter erosion of promises unkept. It is a painful experience that leaves scars not just on the surface but deep within our hearts and minds. When trust is compromised, the foundation of the relationship is shaken, leaving us feeling vulnerable, hurt, and struggling to make sense of what went wrong.

This book is dedicated to those who have faced the daunting task of rebuilding trust after betrayal. Whether you find yourself on the side of the betrayed or the betrayer, the journey ahead is undoubtedly challenging, but it is also a path towards growth, healing, and renewal.

At the core of every healthy relationship lies trust. It is the glue that holds partners, friends, and family members together. When trust is intact, we can be our authentic selves, share our thoughts and feelings openly, and rely on each other's support. However, once trust is compromised, its absence can create a vacuum of doubt, suspicion, and fear. Rebuilding trust isn't merely about restoring things to the way they were; it's about creating a new and stronger foundation that can withstand the storms of life.

Through the chapters that follow, we will delve deep into the intricacies of rebuilding trust after betrayal. We will explore the emotional aftermath of betrayal, the steps to take responsibility for one's actions, the importance of open communication, and the role of patience in the healing process. We will also discuss the significance of setting healthy boundaries, the power of empathy, and the importance of seeking professional help when needed.

It's important to note that this journey is not a linear one. Healing and rebuilding trust is a process that takes time, effort, and a willingness to confront uncomfortable truths. But it is also a journey that can lead to newfound resilience, deeper connections, and a profound understanding of oneself and others.

As we embark on this exploration, remember that you are not alone. Countless individuals have faced the challenges of rebuilding trust, and many have emerged from the experience stronger and more resilient. By arming ourselves with knowledge, compassion, and a commitment to growth, we can begin the process of healing after betrayal and pave the way towards a brighter and more trusting future.

So, let us dive into this journey of renewal and discovery, as we explore the path of rebuilding trust after betrayal – a journey that has the potential to transform pain into strength and brokenness into beauty.

2

Understanding Betrayal

Betrayal is a complex and multifaceted experience that can infiltrate even the most steadfast of relationships. It takes various forms, each leaving a unique imprint on the individuals involved and the bonds they share. In this chapter, we will delve into the different manifestations of betrayal and explore the profound emotional impact it has on both individuals and partnerships.

Forms of Betrayal

Betrayal isn't limited to a single act or circumstance; it can manifest in myriad ways. Infidelity, perhaps the most well-known form, involves breaking the trust and commitment of a romantic partnership. Financial betrayal occurs when one partner hides financial decisions or indulges in secret expenditures that affect both parties. Betrayal can also emerge in the form of broken promises, whether it's failing to follow through on commitments or revealing a confidential matter shared in confidence.

In friendships, betrayal might involve sharing personal information without consent or spreading rumors to the detriment of the relationship. In family dynamics, betrayal can occur when a family member betrays the trust of another, creating rifts that can be challenging to mend.

The Emotional Impact

When betrayal enters the equation, the emotional toll can be overwhelming. For the betrayed, feelings of shock, anger, sadness, and disbelief may surface. The pain can be all-consuming, leading to a profound sense of vulnerability and loss. Trust, once taken for granted, becomes elusive, and individuals grapple with a complex web of emotions that can take a toll on their mental and emotional well-being.

Partnerships, whether romantic, platonic, or familial, are deeply affected as well. The foundations of intimacy and connection are shaken, leaving both parties grappling with questions about the validity of the relationship. Communication can break down, misunderstanding can flourish, and the partnership faces a crossroads – one that leads either to dissolution or the challenging path of rebuilding trust.

As we navigate the treacherous waters of betrayal, it's important to recognize that healing requires acknowledging and addressing these emotions head-on. The emotional impact of betrayal is not a sign of weakness but a testament to the depth of the connection that was once present.

In the subsequent chapters, we will explore strategies to cope with the emotional aftermath of betrayal, including ways to communicate effectively, foster empathy, and work towards rebuilding trust. Remember that understanding the various forms of betrayal and the emotions they evoke is the first step towards the intricate process of healing and renewal.

3

The Importance of Trust

Trust is the invisible thread that binds individuals together in relationships, forming the foundation upon which connections are built. It serves as a cornerstone, supporting the weight of intimacy, vulnerability, and emotional safety. In this chapter, we'll delve into the vital role trust plays in maintaining strong and lasting relationships, and we'll explore the profound effects that broken trust can have on emotional well-being.

The Role of Trust

Imagine trust as a bridge that allows us to traverse the gap between ourselves and others. It enables us to share our thoughts, feelings, and vulnerabilities without fear of judgment or betrayal. Trust empowers us to rely on each other's promises, creating a sense of security that encourages openness and connection. In romantic relationships, trust is the fertile soil in which love can grow, nurtured by faith in each other's intentions and actions. In friendships, trust is the glue that keeps bonds resilient in the face of challenges. Even in professional and familial settings, trust is the lubricant that allows interactions to flow smoothly.

The Effects of Broken Trust

When trust is broken, the impact can be profound and far-reaching. Emotionally, individuals often experience a mix of shock, anger, hurt, and confusion. They may question their own judgment and wonder how they missed the signs of betrayal. The emotional distress can have a ripple effect, causing feelings of anxiety, depression, and even a diminished sense of self-worth.

In relationships, the effects of broken trust can be equally devastating. Partnerships that were once strong may become strained, with both parties grappling to understand what went wrong. The lack of trust can create an environment where communication breaks down, misunderstandings escalate, and intimacy falters.

It's crucial to recognize that the effects of broken trust go beyond the immediate emotional turmoil. They can erode the very fabric of the relationship, making it difficult to regain the sense of safety and connection that once existed.

The Path to Healing

While broken trust can seem insurmountable, the journey to healing is possible. It begins with acknowledging the importance of trust and its significance in relationships. Rebuilding trust involves more than just a return to the status quo; it's an opportunity to strengthen the bonds through transparency, understanding, and growth.

As we move forward in this book, we'll explore the practical steps you can take to rebuild trust after betrayal. We'll delve into strategies for open communication, taking responsibility, gaining insight into motivations, setting healthy boundaries, and nurturing emotional healing. Remember that the process of healing and rebuilding trust is a transformative one, capable of not only restoring relationships but also fostering newfound depth and resilience.

By understanding the role trust plays in our lives and recognizing the impact of broken trust, we can embark on the journey towards healing, renewal, and the reconstruction of relationships that are built on a solid foundation of trust.

4

Taking Responsibility

In the aftermath of betrayal, the road to healing begins with a willingness to take responsibility for one's actions. Acknowledging the harm caused and the pain inflicted is a pivotal step towards rebuilding trust and repairing the damaged relationship. This chapter explores the importance of accountability for the one who caused the betrayal, as well as the role of sincere apologies and genuine remorse in the healing process.

The Importance of Accountability

Accountability is the cornerstone of growth and transformation after betrayal. It involves acknowledging that one's actions had consequences and recognizing the impact those actions had on others. Accepting responsibility is not an admission of weakness, but a demonstration of strength and maturity. By doing so, the person responsible shows a willingness to confront uncomfortable truths and work towards repairing the damage inflicted.

Sincere Apologies and Genuine Remorse

A sincere apology is a bridge that can help mend the breach caused by betrayal.

A heartfelt apology goes beyond a mere acknowledgment of wrongdoing; it expresses genuine remorse and empathy for the pain caused. It demonstrates that the person responsible understands the gravity of their actions and is committed to making amends.

Genuine remorse is the emotional response that underscores the sincerity of an apology. It involves feeling regret for the hurt inflicted, empathizing with the emotions of the betrayed party, and being genuinely sorry for the actions that led to the betrayal. Remorse reflects a desire to change and grow, showing that the individual is committed to learning from their mistakes and preventing further harm.

Navigating the Healing Process

Taking responsibility and offering sincere apologies pave the way for the healing process to begin. However, it's important to note that healing is a two-way street. The person who has been betrayed needs time and space to process their emotions and decide whether they are willing to move forward. Trust cannot be rebuilt overnight, but genuine remorse and accountability lay the foundation for the rebuilding process.

Remember that taking responsibility is a powerful act of rebuilding trust. It signifies a commitment to change, a willingness to learn from mistakes, and a dedication to fostering a healthier relationship moving forward. As we move through this journey of healing after betrayal, keep in mind that accountability and sincere remorse are crucial components in the complex tapestry of rebuilding trust.

5

Rebuilding Communication

Communication is the lifeblood of any relationship, providing the means through which understanding, connection, and trust are nurtured. When trust is shattered by betrayal, communication often takes a hit as well. This chapter delves into the profound impact of broken communication on trust and offers strategies for fostering open and honest dialogue to restore understanding and rebuild the bonds that have been strained.

The Impact of Broken Communication

Betrayal can cause a breakdown in communication between individuals. The sense of vulnerability and hurt can lead to withdrawal, avoidance of difficult conversations, and even the suppression of emotions. In the absence of effective communication, misunderstandings can fester, assumptions can solidify, and mistrust can grow. This can perpetuate a cycle of distance and resentment, making the task of rebuilding trust even more challenging.

Strategies for Restoring Communication

REBUILDING COMMUNICATION

1. Create a Safe Space: Both parties need to feel emotionally safe in order to communicate openly. Establishing ground rules that promote respect, active listening, and non-judgment can create an environment conducive to productive conversations.

2. Be Transparent: Transparency is key to rebuilding trust. Share your thoughts, feelings, and intentions openly. Avoiding half-truths or sugarcoating can prevent further misunderstandings.

3. Active Listening: Listening is as important as speaking. Give your full attention to what the other person is saying. Validate their emotions and show that you are genuinely interested in understanding their perspective.

4. Empathy and Understanding: Put yourself in the other person's shoes. Empathize with their feelings and acknowledge the impact of your actions. This demonstrates your commitment to understanding their experience.

5. Avoid Blame and Defensiveness: Instead of blaming or becoming defensive, focus on owning your part in the situation. Recognize that both parties play a role in communication breakdowns.

6. Ask Open-ended Questions: Use open-ended questions to encourage deeper conversations. This can lead to more meaningful exchanges and help uncover underlying feelings and concerns.

7. Give Each Other Time: Rebuilding communication takes time. Allow each person the space they need to process emotions and thoughts before engaging in conversations.

8. Seek Professional Help: If communication difficulties persist, consider seeking the guidance of a therapist or counselor. A neutral third party can facilitate discussions and provide tools for effective communication.

Moving Forward with Rebuilt Communication

Rebuilding communication is an integral part of rebuilding trust. It requires patience, effort, and a genuine commitment to restoring understanding. Remember that the goal is not just to address the immediate issues but to establish a strong foundation for ongoing, open, and respectful communication. By doing so, you lay the groundwork for the journey towards renewed trust, intimacy, and connection.

As we continue on the path of healing after betrayal, keep in mind that effective communication is a bridge that spans the gap between hurt and understanding. It is a bridge that, when built with care and commitment, can lead to the reconstruction of trust and the renewal of relationships.

6

Gaining Insight into Motivations

Understanding the motivations behind betrayal is a crucial step on the path to healing. It's a journey that requires delving into the depths of one's own actions and emotions, as well as developing empathy for both the betrayer and the betrayed. In this chapter, we explore the significance of gaining insight into motivations and how self-reflection and empathy can contribute to the healing process.

The Need for Understanding Motivations

Betrayal often leaves both parties grappling with questions like "Why did this happen?" and "What led to these actions?" Understanding the motivations behind betrayal is essential because it provides context, allowing both individuals to make sense of the situation. It helps the betrayed individual see that the act was not just a result of random malice, but often a complex interplay of emotions, circumstances, and personal struggles.

For the betrayer, gaining insight into their motivations allows them to take ownership of their actions and uncover underlying issues that may have contributed to their choices. This self-awareness is a powerful tool for personal growth and transformation.

Self-Reflection as a Healing Tool

Self-reflection involves looking inward and examining one's thoughts, feelings, and behaviors. It's an opportunity to dissect the motivations that led to the betrayal and uncover any patterns or triggers. Engaging in self-reflection can be uncomfortable and challenging, but it's an essential step towards understanding one's own actions and taking responsibility for them.

Self-reflection can lead to personal growth, allowing individuals to identify areas for improvement, address unresolved emotions, and develop a deeper understanding of themselves. By acknowledging their own vulnerabilities and flaws, betrayers can work towards becoming more accountable and empathetic individuals.

Empathy: Bridging the Gap

Empathy is a bridge between the betrayer and the betrayed, fostering understanding and compassion. For the betrayed, empathizing with the motivations of the betrayer can lead to a sense of closure and a recognition that actions are often more complex than they seem. This doesn't excuse the betrayal, but it helps in moving towards forgiveness and healing.

For the betrayer, empathizing with the pain and hurt they've caused can be a catalyst for change. It encourages them to view the situation from the perspective of the betrayed, helping them recognize the gravity of their actions and the emotional toll they've taken.

The Healing Power of Understanding

Gaining insight into motivations, engaging in self-reflection, and practicing empathy are all integral to the healing process after betrayal. It's a journey that requires both parties to step into the shoes of the other, examining their own emotions and actions, as well as those of their counterpart. Through this process, the pieces of the puzzle begin to fit together, offering a clearer picture of what happened and why.

As we move forward in our journey of rebuilding trust, remember that gaining insight into motivations is not about excusing or justifying betrayal, but about finding a path towards understanding, growth, and eventual healing. It's a step towards creating a stronger foundation for the future – one built on self-awareness, empathy, and the commitment to becoming better individuals and partners.

7

Setting Boundaries

In the process of rebuilding trust after betrayal, the establishment of healthy boundaries takes center stage. Boundaries serve as protective walls that define the limits of behavior, expectations, and interactions in a relationship. This chapter delves into the significance of setting and maintaining healthy boundaries as a crucial step in rebuilding trust, and how clear expectations and limits can prevent future breaches.

The Role of Healthy Boundaries

Healthy boundaries are the cornerstone of a balanced and respectful relationship. They provide a framework within which both parties can feel safe, respected, and understood. After betrayal, boundaries play a pivotal role in reestablishing a sense of security. They act as guidelines that prevent harmful behaviors, foster open communication, and maintain mutual respect.

Preventing Future Breaches

One of the key functions of boundaries is to prevent the recurrence of actions that led to betrayal. By clearly defining what is acceptable and what is not, individuals can steer away from behaviors that caused harm in the first place. Setting boundaries provides a roadmap for building trust and maintaining a strong foundation for the relationship.

Types of Boundaries

There are several types of boundaries that can be set in a relationship:

1. Physical Boundaries: These define personal space, touch, and intimacy levels. Establishing and respecting physical boundaries is vital for maintaining a sense of comfort and consent.

2. Emotional Boundaries: Emotional boundaries involve sharing feelings, thoughts, and vulnerabilities at a pace that feels right for both individuals. It's about maintaining emotional independence while fostering connection.

3. Time Boundaries: Allocating time for oneself, friends, family, and the relationship is important for balance. Setting clear time boundaries prevents feelings of neglect or suffocation.

4. Communication Boundaries: These determine the manner and frequency of communication. Clear communication boundaries ensure that both parties feel heard without being overwhelmed.

5. Technology and Social Media Boundaries: In the digital age, setting limits on online interactions can help maintain privacy and prevent potential misunderstandings.

Open Communication About Boundaries

Setting boundaries requires open and honest communication between both individuals. It's an opportunity to discuss each other's needs, preferences, and triggers. This conversation should be ongoing, as boundaries may evolve over time. It's important to approach these discussions with empathy and a willingness to understand each other's perspectives.

A Path to Rebuilding Trust

Healthy boundaries are a critical element in rebuilding trust and fostering a resilient relationship. They offer a way to prevent future breaches, create a secure environment, and establish a strong foundation for moving forward. By setting clear expectations and limits, individuals can work together to rebuild trust while cultivating a relationship built on respect, understanding, and mutual growth.

8

Navigating Emotional Healing

The journey of rebuilding trust after betrayal is deeply intertwined with the process of emotional healing. Both the betrayed and the betrayer embark on an emotional journey, navigating complex feelings of hurt, anger, guilt, and vulnerability. This chapter explores the emotional landscape of both parties and discusses techniques for managing these emotions and finding inner healing.

The Emotional Journey of the Betrayed

For the betrayed, the emotional aftermath of betrayal can be overwhelming. Feelings of shock, anger, sadness, and confusion can dominate their experience. The pain may extend beyond the initial discovery, resurfacing in waves as they grapple with the breach of trust. It's essential for the betrayed to acknowledge and validate their emotions, giving themselves permission to grieve the loss of the relationship as they once knew it.

Techniques for Emotional Healing

1. Self-Compassion: Be kind to yourself. Recognize that your emotions are

valid and that healing takes time. Avoid self-blame and practice self-care to nurture your emotional well-being.

2. Seek Support: Reach out to friends, family, or a therapist who can provide a safe space for you to express your emotions and process your feelings.

3. Journaling: Writing down your thoughts and feelings can be therapeutic. It allows you to gain clarity, release pent-up emotions, and track your progress over time.

4. Mindfulness and Meditation: Engaging in mindfulness exercises and meditation can help you stay present and manage overwhelming emotions. These practices promote emotional regulation and self-awareness.

5. Physical Activity: Engaging in physical exercise can release endorphins and help alleviate stress and negative emotions.

6. Art and Creative Expression: Engaging in creative activities such as art, music, or writing can provide an outlet for expressing complex emotions.

The Emotional Journey of the Betrayer

The betrayer, too, experiences a tumultuous emotional journey. Guilt, regret, shame, and a desire for redemption can dominate their thoughts and feelings. They may struggle with the realization of the pain they've caused and the fear of not being forgiven. It's important for the betrayer to confront their emotions head-on and take steps towards making amends.

Techniques for Emotional Healing

1. Self-Forgiveness: Just as the betrayed needs self-compassion, so does the betrayer. Forgiving oneself is essential for personal growth and moving forward.

2. Apology and Accountability: Offering a sincere apology and taking responsibility can provide a sense of closure and contribute to emotional healing.

3. Therapy: Seeking therapy can help the betrayer work through their emotions, understand their motivations, and develop strategies for personal growth.

4. Learning and Growth: Focus on learning from your mistakes and growing as an individual. Channel your guilt into positive change and self-improvement.

5. Communication and Empathy: Engaging in open communication with the betrayed, expressing empathy for their emotions, and understanding the impact of your actions can aid in healing.

The Path to Inner Healing

Both the betrayed and the betrayer must acknowledge that emotional healing is a process. It involves confronting uncomfortable emotions, learning from mistakes, and taking steps towards growth and self-improvement. By employing techniques that promote self-compassion, self-awareness, and positive change, both individuals can embark on the path to inner healing – a journey that paves the way for rebuilding trust, fostering understanding, and eventually finding a new equilibrium in the relationship.

9

Transparency and Honesty

As we navigate the intricate process of rebuilding trust after betrayal, transparency and honesty emerge as guiding stars illuminating the path ahead. This chapter delves into the significance of transparency as trust is rebuilt and discusses how consistent honesty can help rebuild a sense of security within relationships.

The Importance of Transparency

Transparency serves as a powerful antidote to the secrecy and hidden agendas that often accompany betrayal. It involves being open, candid, and forthcoming about one's actions, intentions, and emotions. Transparency is about removing the shroud of uncertainty and doubt that may have clouded the relationship, allowing both parties to see each other clearly and authentically.

Rebuilding a Sense of Security

When trust is broken, a sense of security is compromised. Transparency becomes the cornerstone of rebuilding that security. By being transparent about one's actions and decisions, the person who caused the betrayal demonstrates their commitment to openness and vulnerability. This willingness to be transparent sends a clear message that they have nothing to hide and are willing to be held accountable for their behavior.

For the betrayed, the reassurance of transparency helps in regaining a sense of control and understanding. It allows them to make informed decisions about the relationship's future, based on honest information rather than assumptions or uncertainties.

Consistent Honesty: A Building Block of Trust

Consistency in honesty is key to rebuilding trust. Trust is not restored overnight; it is built gradually through a series of actions and behaviors. Consistent honesty reinforces the message that the betrayer's intentions are aligned with their words. It shows that they are committed to a new path of integrity and that their actions match their promises.

For the betrayed, consistent honesty gradually rebuilds their confidence in the relationship. Each truthful interaction chips away at the doubt that betrayal created, paving the way for the restoration of a strong foundation of trust.

Navigating Challenges in Transparency

While transparency is essential, it's important to navigate the challenges that may arise. Vulnerability can be uncomfortable, and there may be moments when the truth is difficult to share. In such instances, it's important to approach the situation with compassion, recognizing that rebuilding trust is a journey that requires effort and commitment.

A Shared Commitment to Honesty

As we progress in our journey of healing, remember that transparency and honesty are not just individual responsibilities but a shared commitment between both parties. The betrayer must consistently demonstrate transparency, while the betrayed must be open to receiving this transparency with an understanding of the complexity of emotions involved.

Through transparency and honesty, we create an environment where both individuals can rebuild trust and find solace in the shared pursuit of authenticity and understanding. As each truthful interaction unfolds, the bridge to renewed trust grows stronger, leading us closer to the restoration of a relationship grounded in openness, vulnerability, and shared commitment.

10

Patience and Time

In the journey of rebuilding trust after betrayal, patience and time emerge as steadfast companions, guiding us through the intricate process of healing and renewal. This chapter explores the gradual nature of the trust-building process and discusses the indispensable role of patience and the allowance of time for wounds to heal.

The Gradual Process of Trust-Building

Trust, once shattered, cannot be pieced back together hastily. It's a process that unfolds over time, one step at a time. Rebuilding trust requires more than just the resolution to change; it necessitates consistent actions, open communication, and a sincere commitment to growth.

Understanding the Role of Patience

Patience is the cornerstone of the trust-building journey. It's the acknowledgment that healing and rebuilding take time, and rushing the process can undermine the very progress we seek. Patience allows for the space needed to navigate complex emotions, process thoughts, and learn from mistakes.

Both the betrayed and the betrayer must cultivate patience. The betrayed need patience as they navigate their emotions and decide whether to trust again. The betrayer needs patience as they demonstrate consistency, accountability, and a willingness to change.

Allowing Time for Wounds to Heal

Emotional wounds inflicted by betrayal are deep and may take time to heal. Just as physical wounds need time to mend, emotional wounds require space for processing, reflection, and growth. Allowing time for wounds to heal doesn't mean that the journey stagnates; it means that healing is a gradual, transformative process that requires nurturing and care.

Embracing the Process

Patience and time are not adversaries but allies in the journey of rebuilding trust. They offer the opportunity for reflection, personal growth, and the steady accumulation of positive experiences that contribute to the restoration of trust.

Remember that embracing the process of rebuilding trust requires a willingness to be patient with oneself and with the relationship. It's about recognizing that healing cannot be rushed and that the journey is as important as the destination. By embracing patience and allowing time to work its magic, both individuals involved can move towards a future where trust is renewed, bonds are strengthened, and the scars of betrayal become markers of resilience and growth.

11

Chapter 11: Seeking Professional Help

Chapter 11: Seeking Professional Help

In the complex journey of rebuilding trust after betrayal, seeking professional help in the form of therapy and counseling can provide invaluable support. This chapter explores the benefits of turning to trained professionals after betrayal and discusses how their guidance can facilitate the healing process for both the betrayed and the betrayer.

The Benefits of Professional Help

Betrayal can inflict deep emotional wounds that often require specialized care to heal. Therapy and counseling offer a safe and confidential space where individuals can navigate their complex feelings, work through challenges, and gain insights into their emotions and behaviors.

Professional help can be especially beneficial for couples or individuals who are struggling to rebuild trust on their own. Therapists and counselors bring expertise, objectivity, and a wealth of experience to the table, offering tailored guidance that addresses specific needs.

Facilitating Healing and Communication

Therapists and counselors are skilled in facilitating effective communication. They can guide both the betrayed and the betrayer in expressing their emotions, fostering empathy, and understanding each other's perspectives. Through guided conversations, couples can navigate difficult topics, address unresolved issues, and develop strategies for moving forward.

Encouraging Personal Growth

Individual therapy can be immensely beneficial for both parties. For the betrayed, therapy provides a space to process emotions, gain clarity, and develop coping strategies. For the betrayer, therapy offers an opportunity for self-reflection, personal growth, and accountability for their actions.

Learning Tools and Strategies

Therapists and counselors equip individuals with tools and strategies to navigate the challenges of rebuilding trust. They teach effective communication techniques, coping mechanisms for dealing with intense emotions, and methods for fostering empathy and understanding.

A Neutral Third Party

Therapists and counselors act as neutral third parties, creating an environment where both individuals can feel heard and validated. This neutrality prevents power imbalances and ensures that conversations remain constructive and focused on the healing process.

Navigating Difficult Conversations

Certain topics may be too sensitive to address on your own. Professional help provides a structured space for navigating these difficult conversations. Therapists guide individuals through the process, ensuring that emotions are managed and the conversation is productive.

CHAPTER 11: SEEKING PROFESSIONAL HELP

Moving Forward Together

Seeking professional help after betrayal is not a sign of weakness, but a testament to the commitment to healing and growth. Therapists and counselors provide a roadmap for navigating the complex terrain of rebuilding trust, offering guidance, support, and a sense of direction during times of uncertainty.

Remember that the journey of healing after betrayal is not one that needs to be navigated alone. With the guidance of trained professionals, both the betrayed and the betrayer can work towards understanding, healing, and eventually building a stronger foundation of trust and connection.

12

The Journey of Renewed Trust

As we come to the culmination of our exploration into the process of rebuilding trust and healing after betrayal, we find ourselves at a juncture that is both reflective and forward-looking. This chapter delves into the profound journey of renewed trust and offers a synthesis of key takeaways, providing guidance for moving forward in the relationship with newfound understanding and resilience.

Reflecting on the Journey

The journey of rebuilding trust after betrayal is not linear, nor is it without its challenges. It's a journey of self-discovery, growth, and transformation for both the betrayed and the betrayer. Throughout this process, we've explored the intricacies of trust, the impact of broken communication, the role of transparency, the significance of setting boundaries, and the power of patience and time. We've learned the importance of seeking professional help and cultivating empathy and self-awareness.

Key Takeaways

1. Trust is a Process: Rebuilding trust is a gradual process that requires dedication, patience, and consistent effort from both parties involved.

2. Communication is Key: Open and honest communication is essential. It's a bridge that fosters understanding, empathy, and the rebuilding of connections.

3. Transparency and Honesty: Transparency serves as the cornerstone of renewed trust. Consistent honesty reinforces the commitment to change and growth.

4. Setting Boundaries: Healthy boundaries create an environment of respect and security. They prevent future breaches and promote mutual understanding.

5. Emotional Healing: Navigating emotions with patience and self-compassion is integral to the healing process. Seek professional help when needed.

6. Empathy and Self-Reflection: Gaining insight into motivations and cultivating empathy fosters understanding and growth for both parties.

7. Professional Help: Seeking therapy and counseling provides expert guidance, facilitating effective communication and personal growth.

8. Patience and Time: Healing takes time. Patience is essential as wounds heal and trust is rebuilt.

Moving Forward with Renewed Trust

As we move forward, it's important to recognize that the journey of renewed trust doesn't have a defined endpoint. Trust is an ongoing process that requires nurturing and care. Here are some guiding principles for moving forward:

1. Embrace the Journey: Recognize that rebuilding trust is a journey of growth and transformation. Embrace the challenges and triumphs along the way.

2. Practice Patience: Continue to practice patience as trust gradually rebuilds. Understand that setbacks may occur, but they don't negate the progress made.

3. Continued Communication: Maintain open communication and continue to listen, empathize, and understand each other's perspectives.

4. Self-Reflection: Regularly engage in self-reflection to assess your own growth, learn from past mistakes, and ensure that you're aligned with your intentions.

5. Seek Professional Help: If challenges arise, don't hesitate to seek professional help. Therapists and counselors can provide guidance during difficult times.

6. Celebrate Progress: Celebrate the small victories along the way. Each step towards renewed trust is a testament to the dedication and effort invested.

Remember that the journey of renewed trust is a testament to the resilience of relationships and the human spirit. It's a journey that honors the complexities of human emotions, the power of forgiveness, and the capacity for growth. By embracing the lessons learned and the growth achieved, you pave the way for a future built on a stronger foundation of trust, understanding, and connection.

www.ingramcontent.com/pod-product-compliance
Lightning Source LLC
LaVergne TN
LVHW020500080526
838202LV00057B/6077